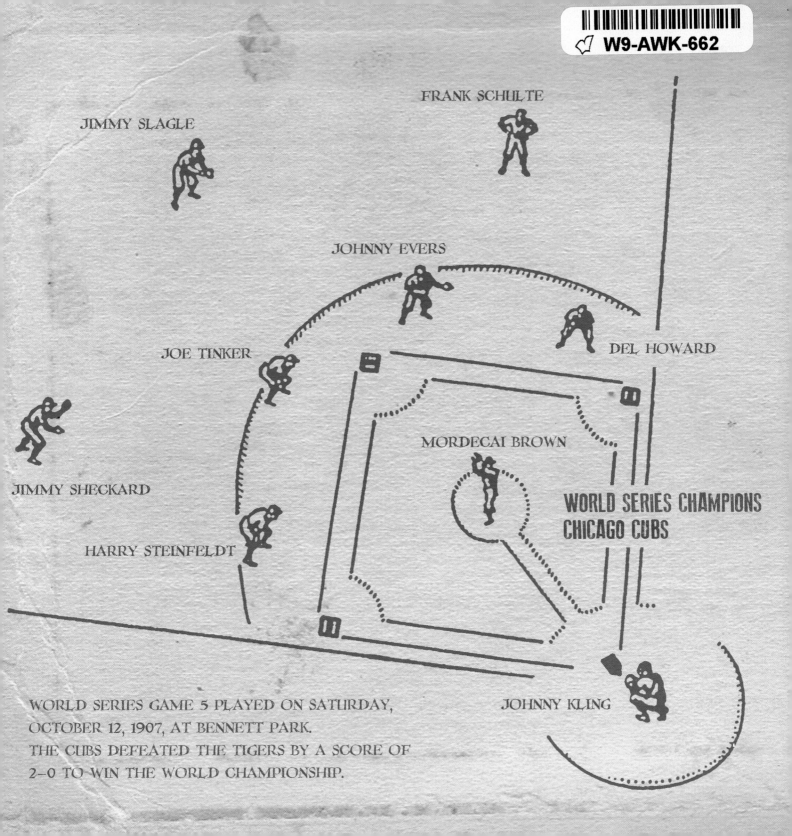

FRANK SCHULTE

JIMMY SLAGLE

JOHNNY EVERS

JOE TINKER

DEL HOWARD

JIMMY SHECKARD

MORDECAI BROWN

**WORLD SERIES CHAMPIONS
CHICAGO CUBS**

HARRY STEINFELDT

JOHNNY KLING

WORLD SERIES GAME 5 PLAYED ON SATURDAY,
OCTOBER 12, 1907, AT BENNETT PARK.
THE CUBS DEFEATED THE TIGERS BY A SCORE OF
2–0 TO WIN THE WORLD CHAMPIONSHIP.

WORLD SERIES CHAMPIONS

CHICAGO CUBS

SARA GILBERT

Published by Creative Paperbacks
P.O. Box 227, Mankato, Minnesota 56002
Creative Paperbacks is an imprint of The Creative Company
www.thecreativecompany.us

Design and production by Blue Design (www.bluedes.com)
Art direction by Rita Marshall
Printed in the United States of America

Photographs by Getty Images (Lee Balterman/Time & Life
Pictures, Bernstein Associates, Jonathan Daniel, Elsa, Michele
Falzone, G. Flume, Brian D. Kersey, Chris McGrath, Ronald C.
Modra/Sports Imagery, National Baseball Hall of Fame Library/
MLB Photos, Photo File/MLB Photos, Rich Pilling/MLB Photos,
Denis Poroy, Louis Requena/MLB Photos, Mark Rucker/
Transcendental Graphics, Jamie Squire, Scott Strazzate/Chicago
Tribune/MCT, Stock Montage, Chris Trotman, Ron Vesely/MLB
Photos)

Library of Congress Cataloging-in-Publication Data
Gilbert, Sara.
Chicago Cubs / Sara Gilbert.
p. cm. — (World series champions)
Includes bibliographical references and index.
Summary: A simple introduction to the Chicago Cubs major league
baseball team, including its start in 1876, its World Series triumphs,
and its stars throughout the years.
ISBN 978-1-60818-261-9 (hardcover)
ISBN 978-0-89812-812-3 (pbk)
1. Chicago Cubs (Baseball team)—History—Juvenile literature. I.
Title.
GV875.C6G54 2013
796.357'640977311—dc23   2011051188

First edition
9 8 7 6 5 4 3 2 1

Cover: Shortstop Starlin Castro
Page 2: Third baseman Ron Santo
Page 3: Pitcher Mark Prior
Right: The Cubs in 1945

1B FRANK CHANCE

1B CAP ANSON

SS ERNIE BANKS

P MORDECAI BROWN

P KERRY WOOD

1B MARK GRACE

TABLE OF CONTENTS

CHICAGO AND WRIGLEY FIELD

Chicago is a big city next to Lake Michigan in Illinois. It is home to a famous ballpark called Wrigley Field. Since 1914, a baseball team called the Cubs has played at Wrigley Field.

RIVALS AND COLORS

The Cubs are a major league baseball team. All the major-league teams try to win the World Series to become champions. The Cubs wear blue, white, and red uniforms. They are **RIVALS** of the St. Louis Cardinals.

PITCHER FERGIE JENKINS

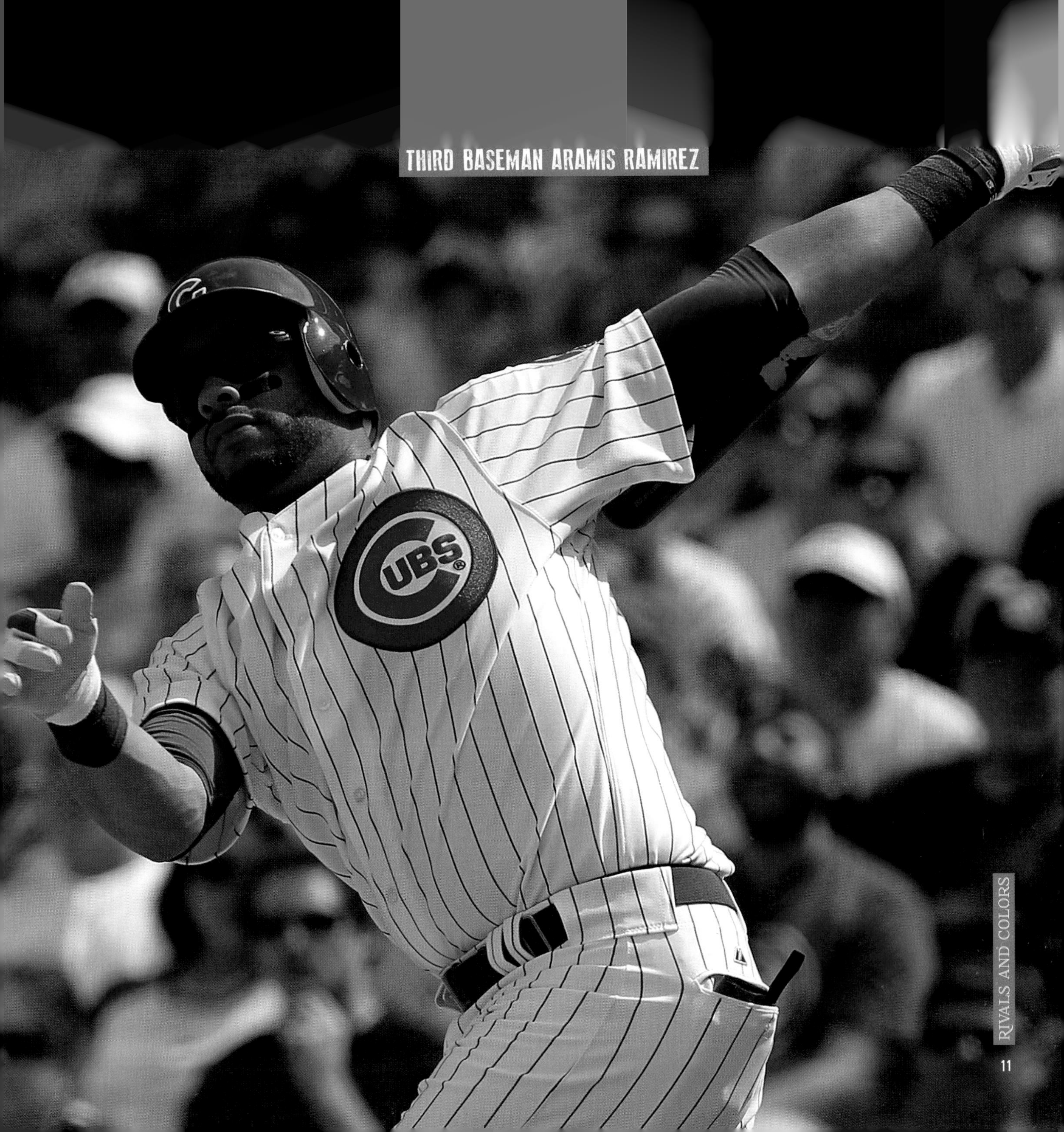

THIRD BASEMAN ARAMIS RAMIREZ

CUBS HISTORY

The Cubs joined the National League in 1876. They were one of the best teams. By 1886, they had won six PENNANTS. In 1907 and 1908, second baseman Johnny Evers helped the Cubs win back-to-back World Series!

Stars like strong outfielder Hack Wilson led the Cubs back to the World Series several

HACK WILSON

CUBS HISTORY

13

2B RYNE SANDBERG

LF ALFONSO SORIANO

P CARLOS ZAMBRANO

3B ARAMIS RAMIREZ

1B DEREK LEE

C GABBY HARTNETT

ERNIE BANKS

times. The Cubs played 14 total games in the 1932, 1935, and 1938 World Series. But they won only two of those games.

In 1945, the Cubs lost the World Series to the Detroit Tigers. The Cubs had some great players after that. Shortstop Ernie Banks won two Most Valuable Player awards. But Chicago did

RIGHT FIELDER ANDRE DAWSON

not get back to the PLAYOFFS for a long time.

Second baseman Ryne Sandberg helped the Cubs reach the playoffs in 1984 and 1989. They made the playoffs in 1998 and three more times after that. But they could not get to the World Series. Fans thought the Cubs were CURSED!

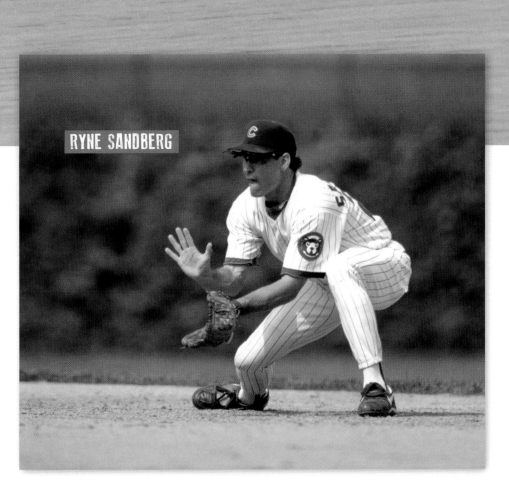

RYNE SANDBERG

BILLY WILLIAMS

SHORTSTOP JOE TINKER

SECOND BASEMAN JOHNNY EVERS

FRANK CHANCE

CUBS STARS

From 1905 to 1912, Frank Chance was the Cubs' first baseman and manager. He led the team to its two World Series wins. Slugging outfielder Billy Williams hit a lot of home runs in the 1960s.

First baseman Mark Grace played for the Cubs from 1988 until

2000. He always worked hard, and the fans loved him. Fans loved outfielder Sammy Sosa, too. Sosa slammed 545 homers for the Cubs.

Shortstop Starlin Castro joined Chicago in 2010. He hit a home run the first time he batted for the Cubs. Fans hope Castro will help the team win a World Series for the first time in more than 100 years!

SAMMY SOSA

PITCHER RYAN DEMPSTER

HOW THE CUBS GOT THEIR NAME

The Cubs were called many different names in their early days. In 1902, the team had many young players. Newspaper reporters started calling them "the Cubs," which are baby bears. The name stuck. The team officially became the Cubs in 1907.

ABOUT THE CUBS

First season: 1876

League/division: National League, Central Division

World Series championships:

1907   4 games to 0 versus Detroit Tigers

1908   4 games to 1 versus Detroit Tigers

Cubs Web site for kids:

http://mlb.mlb.com/chc/fan_forum/kids_index.jsp

Club MLB:

http://web.clubmlb.com/index.html

GLOSSARY

CURSED — stopped from winning or having success by a spell or a kind of bad magic

PENNANTS — league championships; a team that wins a pennant gets to play in the World Series

PLAYOFFS — all the games (including the World Series) after the regular season that are played to decide who the champion will be

RIVALS — teams that play extra hard against each other

INDEX